CAPTAIN IDIOT'S GUIDE to SCHOOL

Are you unintelligent?
Is your shoe size greater than your IQ?
Do you look upon yourself as a bungling biped?

If your answers are
YES YES YES
then what you need is an idiot education!

This book will teach you everything your
teachers don't want you to know. Learn what
idiot schools are really like and impress your friends
with your new-found unintelligence. When you
have finished you will have been transformed
into an educated idiot!

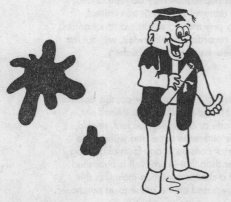

The school librarian thinks this is the
most interesting page in the book.
Idiots always agree with the librarian.
They think ISBN is the school motto:
Idiotus Schoolius Burpius Noisiestus.
The librarian tells them to be quiet.

Copyright © 1992 World International Publishing Ltd.
All rights reserved. Published in Great Britain by
World International Publishing Ltd.,
an Egmont Company, Egmont House, PO Box 111,
Great Ducie Street, Manchester M60 3BL.
Printed in Great Britain.
ISBN 0-7498-1027-0

*A catalogue record for this book is
available from the British Library*

IAN WALSH

ILLUSTRATED BY
HIM ASWELL

World International Publishing
Manchester

IDIOTS WILL NOT UNDERSTAND THIS BIT

This book is dedicated to all the teachers of the world, including Old Mrs Jenkins from down the road who taught her pet hedgehog to head-but flag poles. With special thanks to the King of Iceland.

CAPTAIN IDIOT'S TIMETABLE

MONDAY
2am - MATHS
2·05am - LUNCH
3am - ENGLISH
3·05am - HOME

11am - SCIENCE
11·10am - HOME

7pm - HISTORY
7·01pm - FRENCH
7·02pm - HOME

11pm - GEOGRAPHY
11·06pm - HOME

TUESDAY
1am - BUTTERFLY
COLLECTING
11pm - HOME

WEDNESDAY
4am - SIX HOUR
LECTURE ON
THE ART OF
PEELING
BANANAS
10am - EAT ALL
THE BANANAS
YOU'VE JUST
PEELED
12noon - HOME

THURSDAY
6am - DISSECTION
OF HAIRDRYERS
7am - MANHOLE
STUDYING
10am - TIDDLYWINK
CHAMPIONSHIPS
2pm - DOG DIRT
COLLECTING
8pm - DISCUSSION
ON EAR LOBES
11pm - TREBLE
MATHS

FRIDAY
1am - FREE CLASS
10pm - HOME

SATURDAY
WEEKLY CLASS
EXCURSION TO
THE TOILETS

SUNDAY - DAY OFF !

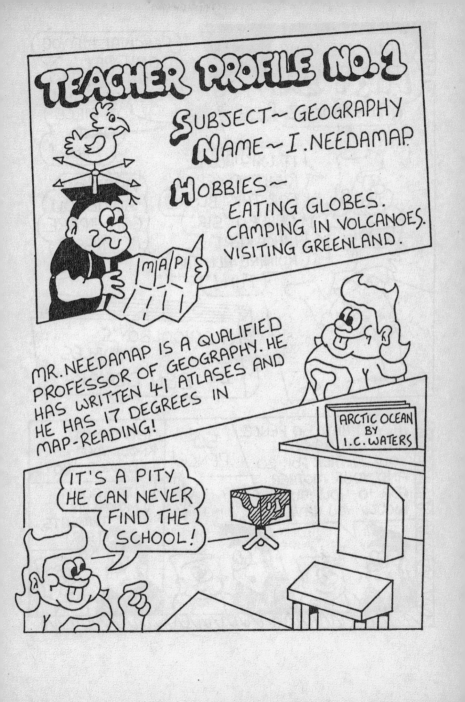

SCHOOL DINNERS

WITH AN IDIOT AS A COOK, MEALS IN IDIOT SCHOOLS ARE EXTREMELY GRUESOME!

IN FACT, SOMETIMES THEY'RE SO DISGUSTING EVEN THE DUSTBINS GET INDIGESTION!

COUGH! COUGH!

AND TO MAKE THINGS WORSE, TODAY WE'RE HAVING COOK'S SPECIALITY— ROAST SWILL!

DINING HALL

ENTER AT YOUR OWN RISK!

BECAUSE THIS SQUARE IS TOO SMALL FOR THE NEXT PICTURE, HERE'S A DRAWING OF A GIANT TOADSTOOL TO KEEP YOU ENTERTAINED WHILE YOU TRY TO FIND THE NEXT PAGE!

MATHS CLASS

NOTHING - TO - DO - WITH - SCHOOL PAGE

WHAT DO YOU CALL A SPANISH FIREMAN?

HOSÉ!

WHAT DO YOU CALL A SPANISH FIREMAN'S BROTHER?

HOSE B!

ELEPHANT JOKES

HOW DO YOU STOP AN ELEPHANT PASSING THROUGH THE EYE OF A NEEDLE?

TIE A KNOT IN HIS TAIL!

WHY DO ELEPHANTS PAINT THEIR FEET YELLOW?

SO THEY CAN HIDE UPSIDE-DOWN IN A BOWL OF CUSTARD!

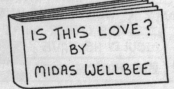

IS THIS LOVE?
BY
MIDAS WELLBEE

HOW DO YOU RECOGNISE AN IDIOT MECHANIC?

HE'S UNDER A WHEELBARROW!

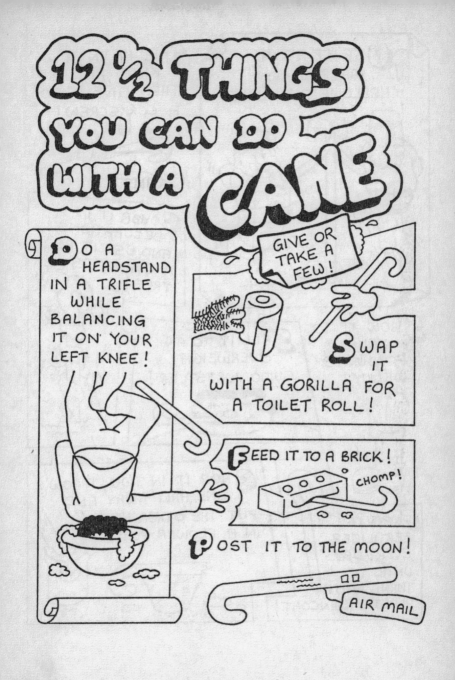

ABSENT FROM SCHOOL

JAMIE, WHY ARE YOU LATE FOR SCHOOL?

WINSTON, YOU WERE ABSENT YESTERDAY. YOU WERE PLAYING FOOTBALL, WEREN'T YOU?

WELL, SIR, I WAS DREAMING ABOUT FOOTBALL! AT EIGHT O'CLOCK, IT WAS 0-0 SO I HAD TO STAY ASLEEP TO SEE EXTRA TIME!

NO, SIR! AND I'VE GOT A JAR OF TIDDLERS TO PROVE IT!

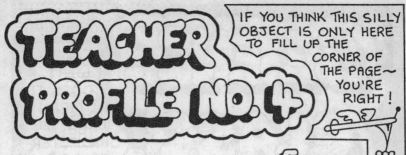

TEACHER PROFILE NO.4

IF YOU THINK THIS SILLY OBJECT IS ONLY HERE TO FILL UP THE CORNER OF THE PAGE~ YOU'RE RIGHT!

SCIENCE TEACHER

AL U. MINIUM

FAMOUS ANCESTORS: HE'S THE 2ND COUSIN ONCE REMOVED OF THE GREAT-GRAND-DAUGHTER OF THE GRAVEDIGGER WHO BURIED THE PET GOLDFISH OF THE APPRENTICE TO EINSTEIN'S PERSONAL MESSENGER!

ACHIEVEMENTS: HE ONCE INVENTED A SANDWICH TOASTER, USING THREE ELASTIC BANDS AND A LARGE BANANA SKIN!

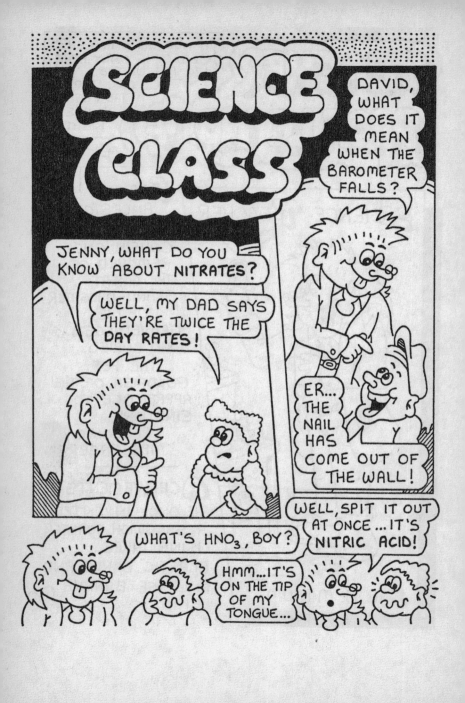

3·00PM

IN THE NEXT STREET, HE FEELS HE HAS TO PRUNE THE TREES!

6·00PM

OLLIES

...AND LATER ON, HE SPENDS AN HOUR CLEANING ALL THE SHOP-FRONTS!

8·00PM

ZOOM!

LŌŌKS AT HIS WATCH, SEES THE TIME AND GOES HOME FOR TEA!

10·00PM

GOES TO BED — TOTALLY EXHAUSTED! THE ENTIRE TOWN IS SPOTLESS BUT THE SCHOOL IS STILL AS FILTHY AS EVER!

AND NOW FOR A JOKE THAT HAS ABSOLUTELY NOTHING TO DO WITH SCHOOL CARETAKERS!

GIVE ME THE FORMULA FOR WATER, BOY!

H, I, J, K, L, M, N, O!

EH?

YOU SAID IT WAS HTOO!

DRAMA CLASS

WHEN I'M OLDER, MY NAME WILL BE IN LIGHTS IN EVERY THEATRE THROUGHOUT THE COUNTRY!

AND HOW ARE YOU GOING TO DO THAT, TRACEY?

I'M GOING TO CHANGE MY NAME TO 'EMERGENCY EXIT'!

TEACHER PROFILE NO. 5

HISTORY TEACHER

R.I.P.

MR. RENÉ SANCE

BORN: A LONG TIME AGO

DIED: A LONG TIME AGO

PARENTS: FOSSIL NO. 1 FOSSIL NO. 2

HE EXPERIENCED EVERYTHING FIRST-HAND!

SCHOOL DEBATE

FRENCH CLASS

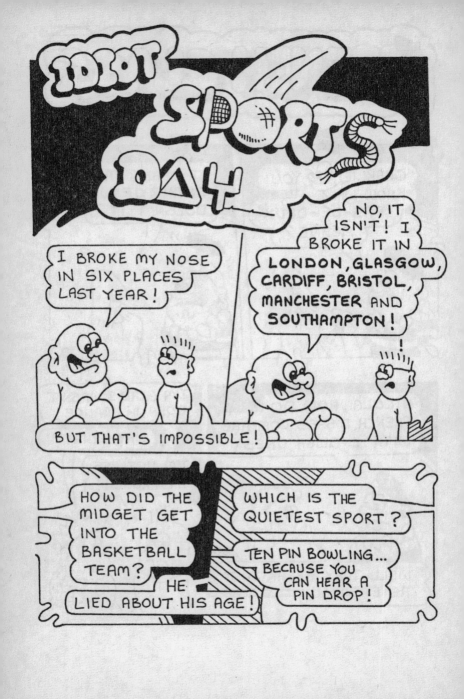

WHAT DO YOU CALL A FLY WITH NO LEGS? A WALK!

PAGES FROM AN IDIOT DICTIONARY

NOT ONLY IS THIS BOOK AN EXCELLENT GUIDE TO IDIOT SCHOOLS, IT IS ALSO A VERY GOOD REFERENCE BOOK...!

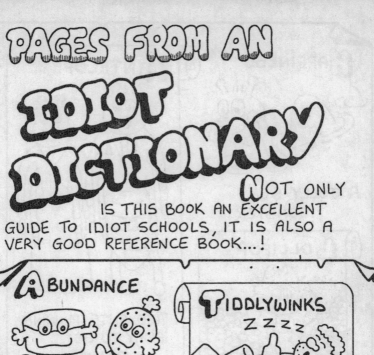

Abundance

A DISCO FOR CAKES

Syllabus

AN IDIOTIC MODE OF TRANSPORT

Tiddlywinks

ZZZZ

A SLEEPING DRUNKARD

Debate

USED TO CATCH DE FISH

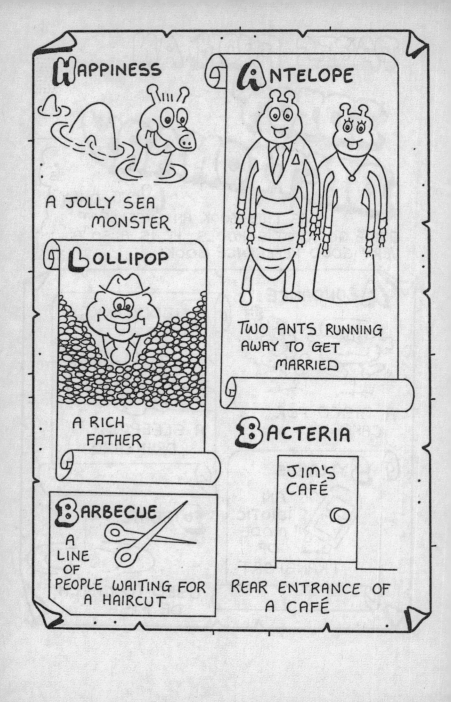

Happiness — A JOLLY SEA MONSTER

Antelope — TWO ANTS RUNNING AWAY TO GET MARRIED

Lollipop — A RICH FATHER

Barbecue — A LINE OF PEOPLE WAITING FOR A HAIRCUT

Bacteria — JIM'S CAFÉ — REAR ENTRANCE OF A CAFÉ

HULLO, READERS! MY NAME IS MISS PASTEL, THE ART TEACHER! TODAY, YOU'RE GOING TO LEARN ABOUT DESIGN AND LAYOUT!

TAKE THIS PICTURE, FOR EXAMPLE! IT IS OBVIOUS THAT THE ARTIST HAS PUT NO THOUGHT WHATSOEVER INTO THE BACKGROUND!

SCHOOL LIBRARY

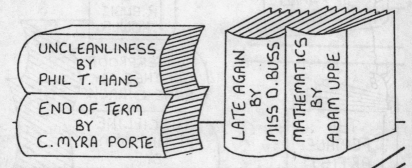

UNCLEANLINESS BY PHIL T. HANS

END OF TERM BY C. MYRA PORTE

LATE AGAIN BY MISS D. BUSS

MATHEMATICS BY ADAM UPPE

MY LIFE AS A MIDGET BY AMMONIA LITTLUN

DOES CRIME PAY? BY LAURA NORDER

GUNFIGHTING BY RICK O'SHEA

ON THE ROCKS BY MANDY LIFEBOAT

THE BAD STRIKER BY MR. GOAL

FIRST IN THE FORM BY HEDDA DE CLASSE

ESCAPE TO THE FOREST BY LUCINDA WOODS

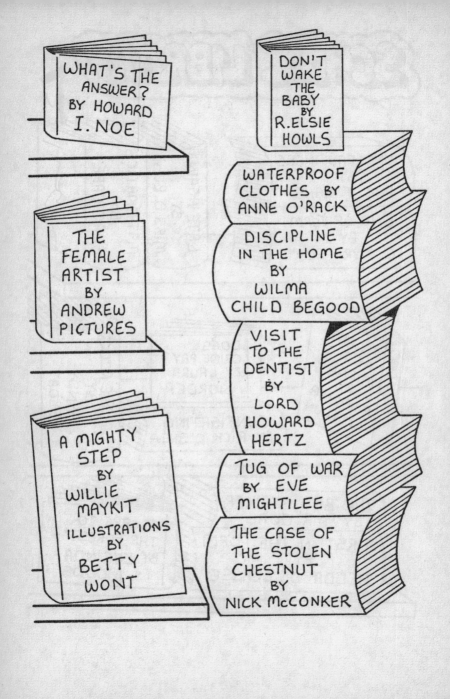

20 THINGS TO DO WITH A MORTAR BOARD

SQUASH IT WITH A GRAND PIANO! **1**

PUT IT ON THE DINNER TABLE AND SIT ON IT! **2**

3 GIVE IT TO A CABBAGE!

4 USE IT AS A TABLE-TENNIS TABLE!

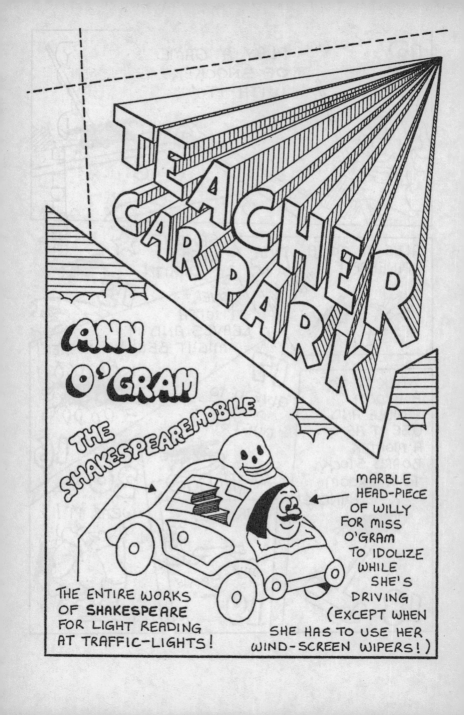

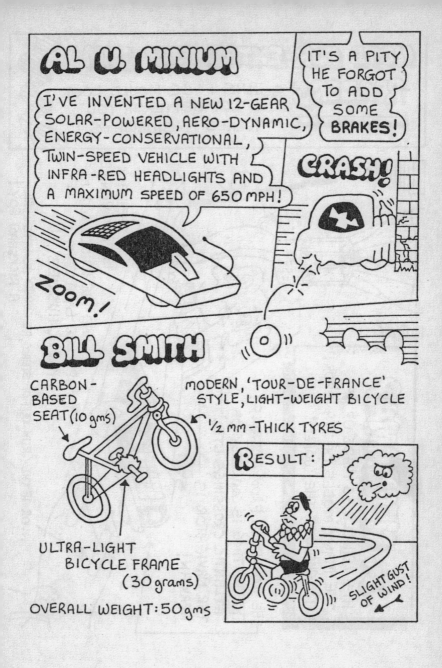

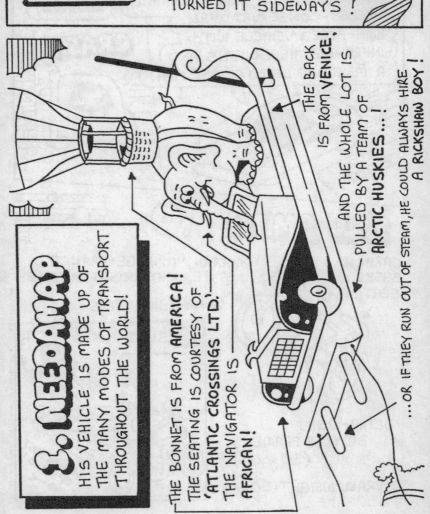

SCHOOL TRIP TO THE MUSEUM

WHAT THE HEAD DOES AT THE WEEKEND

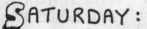

Saturday:

11·00AM

GOES TO THE LOCAL PIG FARM TO PLAY 18 HOLES OF GOLF WITH HIS PET **DRAINPIPE**!

3·00PM

VISITS HIS **GREAT-GRANNY** AND BOTH GO WATERSKIING IN THE **VILLAGE SEWERS**!

8·00PM
PAINTS HIS HAT-STAND **PURPLE** AND GLUES IT TO A REMOTE-CONTROLLED JELLY TEAPOT!

WOBBLE!

SCHOOL MAG

ISSUE NO. 4½

OCTOBER 1991o

MISS O'GRAM INVOLVED IN FIRE

EDITOR:
JOE
BLOGGS

English teacher, Miss Ann O'Gram was involved in a large fire at her home on Smellybreath Street, yesterday afternoon.

Isolated with her young baby on the third floor, she awaited the arrival of the village fire engine.

Once there, the Fire Chief told Miss O'Gram to throw down her baby.

She replied, "I can't! You might drop him", and he then said, "I won't. I'm a trainee goalkeeper!"

With the fire blazing, Miss O'Gram threw down the baby. The Fire Chief caught it perfectly, and has now been appointed goalie of the local Fire Brigade football team. Meanwhile, the younger O'Gram is believed to have joined a toddler's team.

REPORT BY JOE BLOGGS

MATHS TEACHER REFUSED ENTRY TO MUSEUM

EXCLUSIVE BY JOE BLOGGS

Maths teacher, Sir Culsansquares, is reported to have been refused entry to his local museum last week.

An eye-witness told 'School Mag' that they saw Mr. Culsansquares going into the museum and being stopped by an attendant who apparently said, "Please leave your umbrella in the cloakroom". Mr. Culsansquares is believed to have replied, "I haven't got an umbrella". The attendant then said, "I'm afraid you can't come in, sir. I have been given strict instructions not to allow anybody in unless they leave their umbrellas in the cloakroom."

When asked for his statement, Mr. Culsansquares replied, "No comment."

A tremendously angry and irate Sir Culsansquares

Photo: Joe Bloggs

GEOGRAPHY TEACHER ALMOST FINED

BY JOE BLOGGS

MR. NEEDAMAP WAS CAUGHT FISHING IN A PROHIBITED ZONE LAST THURSDAY.

He escaped a £100 fine by convincing the attendant that he wasn't fishing...

he was teaching his pet worm to swim!

Dear Doc

In this section, some of your letters are answered by the 'School Mag' doctor — Dr. I. M. Painless MB BCh Boa PHd GP MD PTO BBC Mc and other piles of letters that mean absolutely nothing whatsoever.

Dear Doc,
   I feel dizzy for half-an-hour after I get up every morning. What should I do?
   _____
Try getting up half-an-hour later.

Dear Doc,
   My hair's falling out. Do you know of anything I could buy to keep it in?
   _____
How about a paper bag?

Dear Doc,
   I've swallowed my mouth organ. What can I do?
   _____
Consider yourself lucky you don't play the piano.

Dear Doc,
   I snore so loudly, I keep myself awake. Can you help me?
   _____
I recommend you sleep in another room.

COMPILED BY JOE BLOGGS

HEADMASTER IN ROW WITH DOCTOR! By Joe Bloggs

Our esteemed headmaster is reported to have had an argument with his local doctor. The incident apparently occurred yesterday afternoon in the village Fish and Chip shop. When asked to comment, the Head said, "I went to the doctor last week with a stomach ache. He told me to drink a pint of apple juice every night after a hot bath. I was simply saying that I had a terrible time trying to drink the bath."

POETRY COMPETITION

After much thought, the panel of judges have decided on a winner for last month's Poetry Competition:

There was a young man from Dundee
Who was stung on the arm by a wasp;
When asked to explain
If he felt any hurt
He said, "No."

BY
Lucy Lastic
Age 7

The winner of second place was the other entrant, Constant Dripping.

'SCHOOL MAG' CROSSWORD BY J.B.

ACROSS:
1. BIG, BLUE WET THING
DOWN: 3rd LETTER OF THE ALPHABET

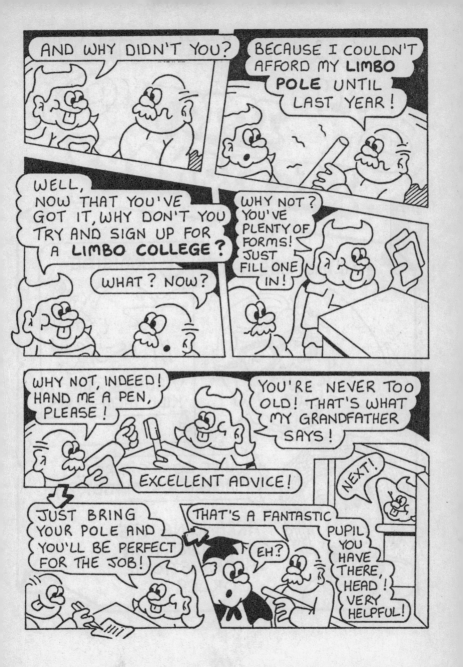

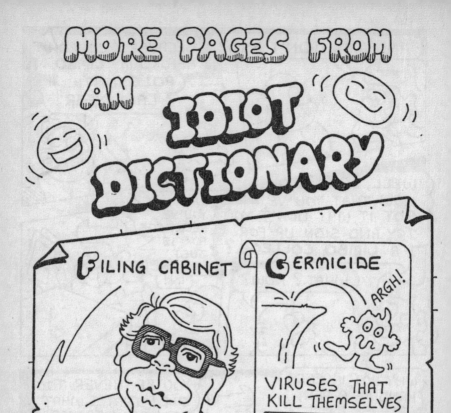

IT'S EXAM DAY

IN SCHOOL TODAY SO I SUPPOSE I'D BETTER GET TO WORK!

SCHOOL EXAM 199█

NAME: _Captain Idiot_ ☺ ∴

ALL QUESTIONS TO BE ANSWERED

1: WHAT'S THE PLURAL OF MOUSE? _Mice_
WHAT'S THE PLURAL OF BABY? _Twins_

2: IF JAM TARTS WERE BEING SOLD AT 20p A DOZEN, WHAT WOULD EACH ONE BE? _Stale_

IDIOT SCHOOL REPORTS

AN EXAMPLE...

IDIOT COMPREHENSIVE

NAME OF PUPIL: Captain Idiot

CLASS: 7th Form

CONTAINING: 24 PUPILS

DATE: CHRISTMAS 19⁕

SUBJECT	MARK	PLACE IN CLASS	COMMENT
MATHS	-5%	24th	Being totally

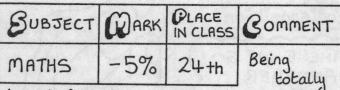

honest, I think a new-born pot-bellied pig from the remote island of Plonk would have a better grasp of Mathematics than your son. **SIGNED:** S.ET. Square

Subject	Mark	Place in Class	Comment
ENGLISH	-10%	26TH (The two class goldfish beat him)	He thinks the word 'negligent' is a man's nightdress!
HISTORY	-5%	LAST!	He obviously didn't bring his brain-cell to the exam!
SCIENCE	0% (CAPTAIN IDIOT'S STRONG SUBJECT)	Second to the left in the third row of desks!	When asked for five members of the cat family, he said, "Mummy cat, Daddy cat and three kittens"!
FRENCH	-20%	2nd best mark (everyone else got 100%)	Translates 'A la carte' as 'By wheelbarrow'!
GEOGRAPHY	-10%	24th	PASS!

COMMENTS FROM HEAD: He's improving! This year he got a total of minus 50%. Last year it was minus 60%. SIGNED:

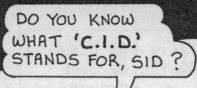

PARENTS' EVENING

NEXT UP WAS **IDIOT THE CONQUEROR** WHO, IN 1066, SHOWED HIS STUDENTS THE EARLIEST FORM OF **FIRE-POWER...**

NOTE THE ADVANCED TECHNOLOGY, STUDENTS!

THROW!

AFTER HIM CAME **IDIOT COLUMBUS**. IT WAS HIS AMBITION TO SAIL TO AMERICA AND TEACH THE NATIVES ALL HE KNEW... AND HE NEARLY DID IT!

KEEP ROWING! WE'VE ALMOST MADE IT!

COME IN, NUMBER NINE, YOUR TIME IS UP!

9

BUT...

9

FINALLY, THERE WERE THE TWINS, **ORVILLE** AND **WILBUR IDIOT**. THEIR FLYING SCHOOL WAS THE FIRST OF ITS KIND...

...AND NO DOUBT THE LAST!

SO YOU SEE, THE QUALITY OF THIS SCHOOL HAS TAKEN YEARS TO EVOLVE!

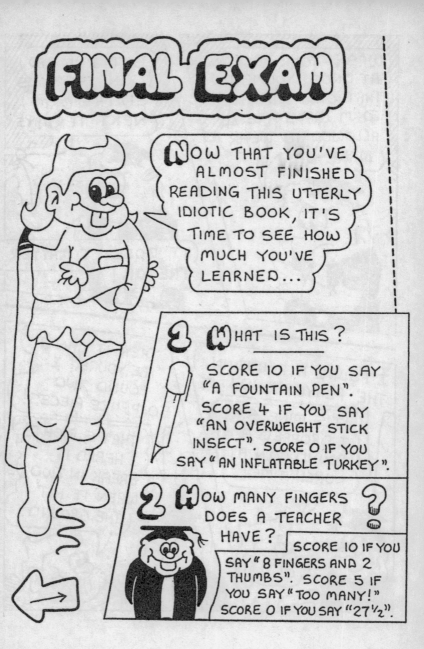

3 WHAT COLOUR IS WHITE CHALK?

SCORE 10 IF YOU SAY "WHITE".
SCORE 5 IF YOU SAY "PURPLE WITH PINK STRIPES".
SCORE 0 IF YOU SAY ANYTHING ELSE!

4 WHEN DO SCHOOLS HAVE THEIR CHRISTMAS HOLIDAYS?

SCORE 10 IF YOU SAY "AT CHRISTMAS".

SCORE 2 IF YOU SAY "EVERY SECOND LEAP YEAR".

SCORE 0 IF YOU SAY "JUST AFTER DINNER!"

5 HOW DO YOU SPELL 'SCHOOL'?

SCORE 10 IF YOU SAY "S-C-H-O-O-L".

SCORE 6 IF YOU SAY "S-K-O-O-O-L".

SCORE 3½ IF YOU SAY "I AM A FISH!"

SCORE 0 IF YOU SAY ANYTHING ELSE!

6 WHAT IS THE MOST POPULAR ANSWER FOR TEACHERS' QUESTIONS?

SCORE 10 IF YOU SAY "I DON'T KNOW".
SCORE 0 IF YOU SAY "I DON'T KNOW".

WHAT WAS YOUR IDIOT GRADE?

SCORE **50-60**: GRADE **F**
SCORE **40-50**: GRADE **E**
SCORE **30-40**: GRADE **D**
SCORE **20-30**: GRADE **C**
SCORE **10-20**: GRADE **B**
SCORE **0-10**: GRADE **A**

CONGRATULATIONS!

YOU HAVE FINISHED READING THIS BOOK WITHOUT EATING AN ARTICULATED LORRY, FLUSHING AN ARMCHAIR DOWN THE TOILET OR GOING TOTALLY CUCKOO IN ANY OTHER WAY. TO SHOW THIS ACHIEVEMENT, FILL IN THIS DIPLOMA, CUT IT OUT AND HANG IT IN YOUR ROOM!

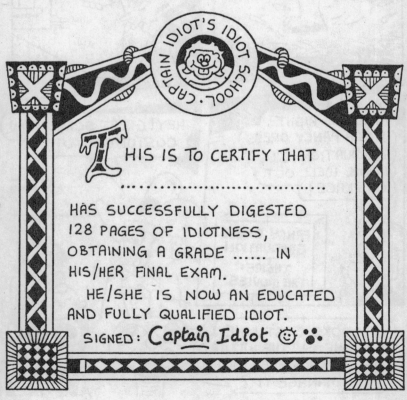

CAPTAIN IDIOT'S IDIOT SCHOOL

THIS IS TO CERTIFY THAT

....

HAS SUCCESSFULLY DIGESTED 128 PAGES OF IDIOTNESS, OBTAINING A GRADE ...... IN HIS/HER FINAL EXAM.

HE/SHE IS NOW AN EDUCATED AND FULLY QUALIFIED IDIOT.

SIGNED: Captain Idiot ☺ ⁘